BRILLIANT BLAWGS

A BRÜTAL PIXIE PUBLICATION

ALSO BY LETICIA

*Music Journalism 101: The definitive
resource for new and established writers*

The Art of Postcard writing

BRILLIANT BLAWGS

A PLAYBOOK FOR **CREATING AND MAINTAINING STRATEGIC BLOGS** THAT CLIENTS & PROSPECTS LOVE

BY LETICIA MOONEY

Brilliant Blawgs: A playbook for creating and maintaining strategic blogs that clients and prospects love.

ISBN 978 099 2283735.

This work was first published in 2017.

Published by Brutal Pixie Pty Ltd ATF the Pixie Trust.
PO Box 1190
Pasadena SA 5042
AUSTRALIA

Email: hello@brutalpixie.com
Call: +61 8 8121 4134

Cover art and typesetting by Stacey Grainger. Page design by Brutal Pixie.

Contents

Introduction

With this playbook, you are one step closer to a meaningful and effective blog for your law firm. Before you dive in and get started, block off ten minutes for this introduction. While it only takes three-and-a-half minutes to read, you will probably want four or five minutes to think about it and two minutes make a few notes.

Why do you want to create an effective blog for your law firm?

It's true that content is what drives the internet. It is also true that if your motivation for blogging is because your competitors are, because it seems like the 'in' or 'right' thing to do, or because your SEO guy told you to, that this resource is will be a waste of your valuable time.

If your reason is legitimately one of those, please email us at hello@brutalpixie.com and tell us that you bought it too soon, and we will refund you every cent of the purchase price. You get to keep the playbook.

No, that's not a joke. This playbook is only going to be effective for you if your law firm's strategy is much more than keeping up with the Joneses.

When your strategy is because they are, or because someone said so, it's an indication that your firm's business hasn't evolved to the point where you can sustain any kind of publishing activity without problems.

Those problems include other team members moaning about it being difficult, hard work, expensive, or (insert any other complaint here). The on-flow effect is that subject-matter experts delay their reviews, approvals are hard to obtain, and changes are continuous, painful, and annoying. The complaints that you will hear occur because you don't have a clear corporate strategy in place, one that has defined and specific customer and communication elements for which blogging is an identified and necessary activity. In other words, when your team members ask you why you're doing this, your reason won't be because we feel like we should or because they are or because our SEO guy told us to.

Phew! It's a hard way to get into a resource like this isn't it? Hopefully you are still here and haven't asked for your $199 back.

What do you imagine could be the result of your blogging?

Really think about this. Imagine it. Visualise it. Feel what it's like to see it come to life. Inspirational, isn't it? A word of caution is wise here. If you think that by blogging you will get hundreds more people visiting your website, you are more than likely going to be disappointed. A blog is only one element of a successful marketing strategy. Doing it well is going to be more successful for you than doing it badly, but it's still only one part of a more complex whole.

The vision of the result gives you an indication as to the purpose of your blogs. If the result is leads, then the purpose is to deliver enough value to someone that they exchange their personal information with you. If the result is to be a thought leader, then perhaps the purpose is to create shareable or provocative material, enough to provoke responses of some kind. If the result is to sell a service, perhaps the purpose is to demonstrate the value of your firm as that service's provider.

Each purpose yields different topics, different styles, and even different types of content. Thought leadership means commentary on topical issues, with a depth of knowledge and research. Demonstrations of value as a service provider mean case studies, examples, and lessons that you can draw from your experience.

So what is blogging done well?

A good blog is one that is consistent, has a purpose and an intention, has a clear reader, and adds value to that reader.

Secondarily, a good blog may also be one that is shared, that generates leads (meaning you also need something to offer people as part of blog-as-package idea), and that helps to position your firm as a leader or authority in your discipline. 'Good' here equates to 'success' and can (and should) be measured.

The secondary elements are ones that you can measure financially. But if the downloads attached to your blogs are of value to your readers, then you may decide to measure 'value' by the number of downloads or leads generated, too.

Know that your consumers are sensitive to value

Your primary goal is to add value to someone else, for free. This apparent reversal of commerce is what trips up so many firms in the legal profession. It has happened because the nature of commerce has changed. Consumers are sensitive to the value they are getting from their vendors, and as a law firm, you are only another vendor.

When your consumers are sensitive to value, so must you be. You must also be prepared to demonstrate up-front that you are worth their trust. The days of the legal profession being able to rest on its nature as a 'profession' are long gone. Happily, adapting is easy if you're prepared to think about putting your clients and not-yet-clients in front of you.

Ready? Let's go

This playbook gives you the rules and tactics that you can deploy to take advantage of the new economy. Let's get started.

Get the most out of this book

Understanding the components in this book will help you get the most out of it. It will help you set the right expectations.

Navigation & Symbols

Each page has a box near the top that gives you time estimates, and an indication of progress. It shows you precisely where you are in the process, and tells you how much more is left.

Time to read

Time to prepare

Time to do

Progress indicators

Blogging is a process, so it helps to know whereabouts each step fits into that process. That's why this Playbook has progress indicators at each step.

Green smileys tell you how much you've completed.

Yellow smileys tell you what is currently 'in progress'.

Grey smileys tell you how many more steps remain.

Understand the 'shape' of the process

All content projects have the same shape or feel when the correct process is followed. The shape is the same when you are editing books as it is when you are publishing blogs.

This 'shape' is what they feel like to work on:

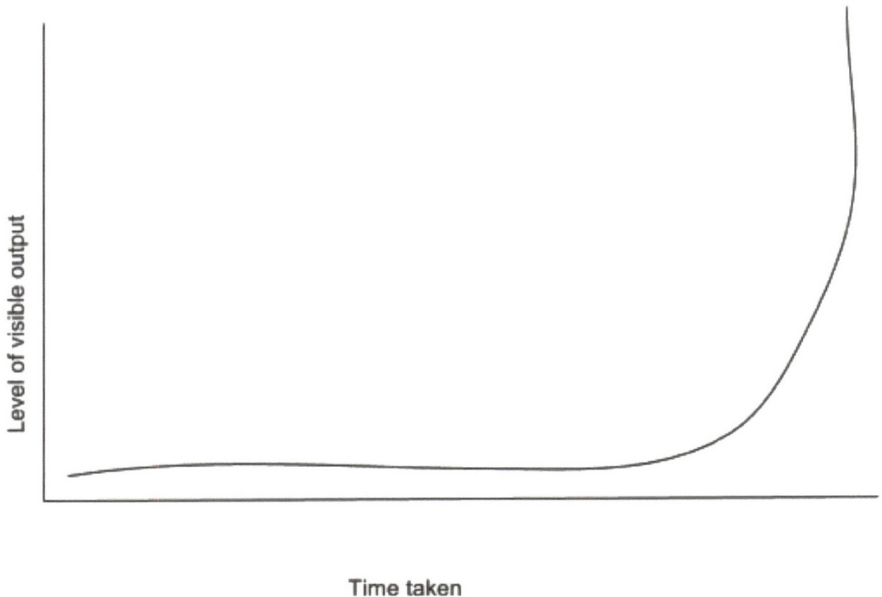

Level of visible output

Time taken

In other words, they feel like you are doing a lot of things without any end result, until all of a sudden - whoosh! - it's all in place. Know this from the outset, know that it's how the process works, and be comfortable with it.

The internet makes us believe (falsely) that everything happens, or should happen, quickly. Even the most 'reactive' content producers - such as news outlets - can only react because they prepared materials earlier.

Set the right foundation

Make sure that your blogging supports your corporate strategy. Strategic alignment is important when you undertake any communication activity, and blogging is no exception to that rule. Everything your business does, it should do for a reason.

🙂🙂🙂🙂🙂🙂🙂🙂🙂🙂

🕐 2 mins   📋 5 mins   ✏ 15 mins

Mission, Vision, Intention

Step one is to be clear about the mission, vision and intention of your firm.

If your firm is a generalist firm, and therefore has a number of different areas that it services, defining your intention may either (a) be more difficult to write, or (b) be multifaceted.

Which one this is depends on the level of complexity. If each division operates singly, and you struggle to create a unifying intention, step down to each area level. Be aware that this means that you will be better served by segmenting your communications, so you don't muddy your message.

Preparation

If you already have mission and vision statements, go and find them before you start.

> *Intention Writing: Pro Tip! - Structure*
>
> [FIRM NAME]
> intends to [TAKE THIS ACTION]
> for [THIS TYPE OF CLIENT OR GROUP]
> by [THIS DATE OR YEAR].

ACTIVITY: Fill in the blanks!

What is the mission of your law firm?

_____

_____

_____

_____

_____

What is the vision for your firm?

Three years:

_____

_____

_____

_____

_____

Five years:

_____

_____

_____

_____

Ten years:

_____

_____

_____

_____

What is your firm's intention?

_____

_____

_____

_____

_____

_____

Set the right foundation

Worked Example

Let's imagine that you and I have our own firm. It's a firm that works in environmental law. And it's called Organic Justice.

The **Mission** of Organic Justice is to represent the environment in all issues where it could and should have a voice, so that humanity doesn't come to regret its developments.

The **Vision** of Organic Justice is to fight successfully to preserve the integrity of natural spaces where development is damaging to the ecosystems that support life, and to be a key provider of environmental law education for non-lawyers.

Organic Justice **intends to** successfully represent the environment in ten major industrial and/or developmental cases in the South Pacific region annually.

How this helps you

Establishing your mission, vision and intention like this gives you a high-level publishing brief.

Drawing on the worked example above, we know that any publishing that Organic Justice undertakes must:

- Have an educational component
- Demonstrate success somehow, potentially via case reviews, news releases, or videos that show joy at successful outcomes

- Have topics that include industrial development, 'other' developments (maybe they are residential? We'd need to find out), ecosystems that support life, natural spaces, the role of law in these cases, past cases where the environment wasn't represented and the damaging outcomes.

We also know that whatever Organic Justice does, it must also publish commentary on topical developments or cases in which the firm is not involved, but that are in the press.

As a starting point, this is has greater clarity than just 'diving in'. It shows you that the firm already has a significant brief. And this is before we get to the audience, to the corporate strategy, or a market assessment.

In the next section, we take a deeper dive into the landscape and find out what your competitors are doing (so you can avoid doing that too).

Competitive Analysis

You need a competitive analysis so you understand what else your readers might be exposed to. In any business, understanding options, alternatives, and competition is critical if your company is going to be successful. Blogging is no exception to this, because everybody wants attention.

☺️☺️☺️☺️☺️☺️☺️☺️☺️☺️

🕐 **2 mins**   📋 **60 mins**   ✏️ **90 mins**

Start with research

To find out what's available out there, you need to do two kinds of research. The first is to find out what your **direct competitors** are doing. The second is to find out what **your alternatives** are doing.

An alternative is a firm that doesn't do exactly what you do but is close enough. A direct competitor does pretty much exactly the same thing as you do. The reason alternatives are important is self-evident when you think about how you buy in to things: Sometimes you'll settle for an alternative if it appears to be kind-of-right.

Gather data

To gather data, set up a table or spreadsheet and go hunting. Set a timer for an hour, and then go hunting. No matter what happens, don't spend more than an hour.

On the next page is a sample table that you may choose to use.

Analyse data

Data analysis is only as good as the questions you ask of your data. With this in mind, your goal with your data analysis is to emerge with a list of topics, readers, and sequences that are already out there on the internet. It needn't be any more complicated than the topics list you saw in the worked example.

The best way to get to this point is to throw everything on a whiteboard, or define a set of colours for each topic and map them out. Ideally, you will unearth a list of topics, and will understand which ones are published more often than the others.

Then, if there are specific questions that any of the blogs address, you want to know those as well. It could be that they are questions that people actually ask of the firm, but it is much more likely that they are questions the other providers just 'thought up'.

Use the tables on the next two pages to keep clean copies.

Competitive Analysis

Competitor			
Blog Topics			
Describe the intended reader (age, gender, demographic)			
What questions do blogs answer?			
How often are they published?			
What pattern do blogs follow?			

Competitive Analysis

Results Analysis: Topics

Rank Topics (most to least published)	List all the *specific* questions they answer

Competition: Pro Tip! - Gaps

The best opportunity for YOUR publishing is in the gaps left behind by everyone else.
Repeating what they do = failure.

Competitive Analysis

Results Analysis: Sequencing

Do your competitors & alternatives publish on the same cycle? Can you do something different?

Sequences: Most to least common	Frequency pattern: Most to least common

Results Analysis: Ideal Readers

Know who your competitors are talking to. It's likely that their audience is not your audience.

Ideal Reader 1: Profile	Ideal Reader 2: Profile

The right material for the right person

It is very common to see law firms targeting 'everyone'. If you are tempted to do this, a word of warning: It doesn't work.

☺☺☺☺☺☺☺☺☺☺

🕐 1 mins   📋 0 mins   ✒ 15 mins

Talk to everyone, get nobody

Aiming for 'everyone' in business doesn't work, aiming for 'everyone' in content doesn't work. The reason is because when you have a specific person in mind, you attract people like them.

It's even more important to define your target when it comes to content.

Here is why:

- It makes writing much easier.
- It sets the tone and the language.
- It sets the types of downloads you offer.
- It sets the style, the function, the format.
- It enables you to test easily.

ACTIVITY: Your ideal reader

Age: _____

Education level: _____

Languages: _____

Occupation: _____

Likes: _____

Dislikes: _____

Fears: _____

Reads/watches: _____

Listens to: _____

Location: _____

Income: _____

Family life? _____

Hobbies: _____

Holidays in: _____

Uses what device? _____

Lifestyle quirks: _____

Strategy statement

While blogging is a continuous activity, it still has intended outcomes, in the same way that projects do. To help you get closer to your outcomes, you can define a strategy statement.

☺☺☺☺☺☺☺☺☺☺

🕐 **1 mins**   📋 **5 mins**   ✏ **15 mins**

About strategy statements

All listed companies have strategy statements. They are less common in the legal profession, in which businesses tend to be partnerships rather than companies.

Strategy statements come after your mission, vision, and intention, and even after your values. Viewed in a list of corporate statements (mission, vision, intention, values), think of it as sitting at around number five.

What the strategy statement contains

- Your outcomes, or what you want to achieve in a specific timeframe.
- The scope, or what part of your business landscape this occupies.
- The competitive advantage, or how you will do things differently from, or better than, the competition.

Now you know why the competitive analysis had to be done before you got to your strategy statement!

Craft your blog publishing strategy statement

This is what your statement ought to look like:

We want to achieve this outcome] in [this timeframe] or by [this date] for [this person].

Knowing that the scope of topics includes topics from intention, mission, vision], our blog occupies [this part of our business landscape].

We will carve our own niche and separate ourselves from the competition by focusing on [these topics and types].

Now, write yours:

_____

_____

_____

_____

_____

_____

_____

_____

_____

_____

Success Measures

In your strategy statement you included a list of outcomes. Success measures tell you that you have achieved your outcomes. If you don't have the right measure, you won't know whether you've achieved them.

☺☺☺☺☺☺☺☺☺☺   🕐 **1 mins**   📋 **0 mins**   ✏ **15 mins**

Types of measurement (metrics)

The metrics that you will use will depend entirely on your intention and your intended outcomes.

There is no one-size-fits-all measurement structure. If there were, then everyone's publishing would be run-of-the-mill. It's no secret that this is why so much 'cookie-cutter' (noise) content exists: That content isn't strategic

When metrics work to support your direction, they are specific to your publishing. This means they are specific to *your* topics, *your* goals, *your* outcomes.

ACTIVITY: Think about metrics

In the space below, make some notes about how each of the metrics on the right-hand side demonstrate success. What might they mean for you?

Map metrics to your outcomes

METRIC	INDICATES
Views	Number of individual visitors.
Visit time	How engaging it is (< 30 sec indicates no engagement). Also whether people read all of it or just some of it (5 min versus 2 min).
Comments	Engagement, provocation.
Shares	Value to the reader.
Downloads	Engagement & value, also warm leads.

Success Measures

Identify your own specific metrics

Following the earlier example, add metrics specific to *your* publishing activity.

Metric	What it indicates	Which of your outcomes does it relate to?	How does it demonstrate success?

Accountability

The most common reason for the failure of publishing projects is lack of accountability. Accountability is not a pretty word. It says that if you fail to do something, there are consequences.

🕐 **4 mins**   📋 **0 mins**   ✏️ **60 mins**

Why is accountability scary?

It's not pretty, but there should be consequences. You wouldn't be in this section right now if you hadn't determined that publishing is a critical part of delivering on your strategic plan. Therefore, failing to be accountable for the work means you're not serious about your strategy.

It's scary. It's also easy to put in place, and easy to get right.

Accountability is about *people*, not *roles*

Instead of seeing accountability as judgemental key performance indicators, it's better to use it as leverage for staff development.

When you use it this way, accountability becomes a way for you to engage all parties in a workflow, and also to assess and assign capabilities and skill-sets that your firm might not otherwise provide.

How to assign accountability in five simple steps

The simplest method is known as the W.R.A.C.I. framework. (We pronounce it, *racy*. Oo er.)

STEP 1. Define the production flow

If you already produce content, a workflow map is valuable to you. If your publishing isn't active yet, you need to design the flow.

Think carefully about subject-matter experts and their roles. Key revenue earners are better kept to review for fact-checking and accuracy only, rather than editorial work. Here's an example flow:

- Define topics
- Approve topics
- Define media required
- Set publishing schedule
- Set approval schedule
- Set design/image sourcing/creation schedule
- Set drafting schedule
- Set researching schedule
- Assign topics to researchers, writers, designers
- Load into content management system Add metadata
- Schedule the article to go live on the right date.

Accountability

STEP 2. Decide who is responsible for each piece of work.

What	Who is Responsible? Think: *People*, not *roles*	
	Example	Who in your firm is responsible?
Define topics	*John*	
Approve topics	*Nancy*	
Define media required	*Stella*	
Set publishing schedule	*John*	
Set approval schedule	*John*	
Set desing/image sourcing/creation schedule	*Stella*	
Set drafting schedule	*John*	
Set researching schedule	*John*	
Assign topics to researchers, writers, designers	*John*	
Research conent	*Holly*	
Write content	*Holly*	
Approval 1: Subject-matter expert review	*Nancy*	
Approval 2: Editorial check	*John*	
Load into content management system	*Ben*	
Add metadata	*Ben*	
Schedule the article to go live on the right date.	*Ben*	

Accountability

STEP 3. Decide who is accountable for each activity.

What	Who is Responsible? Think: *People*, not *roles*	
	Example	**Who in your firm is responsible?**
Define topics	*Nancy*	
Approve topics	*Sam*	
Define media required	*John*	
Set publishing schedule	*John*	
Set approval schedule	*Nancy*	
Set desing/image sourcing/creation schedule	*John*	
Set drafting schedule	*Nancy*	
Set researching schedule	*Nancy*	
Assign topics to researchers, writers, designers	*Nancy*	
Research conent	*John*	
Write content	*John*	
Approval 1: Subject-matter expert review	*Sam*	
Approval 2: Editorial check	*John*	
Load into content management system	*Hester*	
Add metadata	*Hester*	
Schedule the article to go live on the right date.	*Hester*	

Accountability

STEP 4. Decide who needs to be engaged in active communication for each activity

| What | Who is Responsible? Think: *People*, not *roles* | |
	Example	Who needs to be engaged in communication?
Define topics	*Holly, Stella*	
Approve topics	*John*	
Define media required	*Holly*	
Set publishing schedule	*Holly, Stella, Ben, Hester*	
Set approval schedule	*Nancy*	
Set desing/image sourcing/creation schedule	*Stella*	
Set drafting schedule	*Holly*	
Set researching schedule	*Holly*	
Assign topics to researchers, writers, designers	*Holly*	
Research conent	*Nancy*	
Write content	*Holly*	
Approval 1: Subject-matter expert review	*Nancy*	
Approval 2: Editorial check	*Holly*	
Load into content management system	*Ben*	
Add metadata	*Ben*	
Schedule the article to go live on the right date.	*Ben*	

Accountability

STEP 5. Decide who needs to be kept informed?

What	Who is Responsible? Think: *People*, not *roles*	
	Example	**Who needs to be kept informed?**
Define topics	*Nancy*	
Approve topics	*Holly, Stella, Nancy*	
Define media required	*Nancy*	
Set publishing schedule	*Sam*	
Set approval schedule	*Ben, Hester*	
Set desing/image sourcing/creation schedule	*Holly*	
Set drafting schedule	*Stella*	
Set researching schedule	*Stella*	
Assign topics to researchers, writers, designers	*Sam*	
Research conent	*John*	
Write content	*John*	
Approval 1: Subject-matter expert review	*Holly*	
Approval 2: Editorial check	*Sam*	
Load into content management system	*John, Hester*	
Add metadata	*Sam*	
Schedule the article to go live on the right date.	*Sam, Nancy, John*	

Accountability

Complete your Accountability Matrix

Congratulations! You now have a complete WRACI matrix. All you have to do now is put it into one specific table, then make sure everyone is on board.

If you have a tech team and tech environment capable of handling it, you can now configure automatic notifications based on this accountability matrix.

What	Responsible	Accountable	Communicated to	Informed
Define topics	John	Nancy	Holly, Stella	Nancy
Approve topics	Nancy	Sam	John	Holly, Stella
Define media required	Stella	John	Holly	Ben
Set publishing schedule	John	John	Holly, Stella, Ben, Hester, Nancy	Sam
Set approval schedule	John	Nancy	Holly	Ben, Hester
Set desing/image sourcing/creation schedule	Stella	John	Ben	Holly
Set drafting schedule	John	Nancy	Holly	Stella
Set researching schedule	John	Nancy	Holly	Stella
Assign topics to researchers, writers, designers	John	Nancy	Holly	Sam
Research conent	Holly	John	Nancy	John
Write content	Holly	John	Nancy	John
Approval 1: Subject-matter expert review	Nancy	Sam	Holly	John
Approval 2: Editorial check	John	John	Holly, Nancy	Sam
Load into content management system	Ben	Hester	John, Holly, Nancy	Hester
Add metadata	Ben	Hester	John, Holly	Sam
Schedule the article to go live on the right date.	Ben	Hester	John	Sam, Holly

Then what? - Workflow

What comes after publishing?

There is another stage beyond publishing, which is the distribution or marketing of your content. That is not covered in this playbook. Be aware that the lines of responsibility and accountability for that may influence who needs to be informed about production.

Every element of workflow has an input and an output. Spending time thinking about the place that publishing has between those two elements is worth every minute you spend on it.

bonus!

FREE
Content strategy
consultation

CODE: Plb00k17

Book at http://bit.ly/2ljMlwX

Accountability

Accountability Matrix template

What	Responsible	Accountable	Communicated to	Informed
Define topics				
Approve topics				
Define media required				
Set publishing schedule				
Set approval schedule				
Set desing/image sourcing/creation schedule				
Set drafting schedule				
Set researching schedule				
Assign topics to researchers, writers, designers				
Research conent				
Write content				
Approval 1: Subject-matter expert review				
Approval 2: Editorial check				
Load into content management system				
Add metadata				
Schedule the article to go live on the right date.				

Risk Thinking

De-risking your publishing activity is hopefully something about which you get excited. If it's not, it should be!

🙂🙂🙂🙂🙂🙂🙂🙂🙂🙂

🕐 **3 mins**   📋 **0 mins**   ✏️ **60 mins**

Risk has a bad name. But de-risking something means that you know your publishing activity is:

- Suitable
- Appropriate
- Useful and helpful to your clients (and not-yet-clients)
- Supportive of your brand
- Supportive of your strategy
- Supportive of your people.

Lawyers are great at assessing risk before leaping. This means that weaving risk thinking into all of your publishing activity will be somewhat natural to you. Great news!

Elements you could add to your risk assessment

There are a number of elements to add to your risk assessment. They include:

- Operational risk: Absences, delays, workflow bottlenecks
- Content risk: Errors, off-brand voice, off-topic publishing
- Technology risk: Failure, penetration attack, vendor failure, content blocking

- Compliance risk: Advice vs information, contravention of Law Society guidelines
- Professional risk: Complaint to Law Society by another firm

Create a risk scoring system

You may already have a risk scoring system in your business. If you have, use it here to assess the risks in front of you.

If you don't have a risk scoring system, there is one you can use on the following page.

Each risk needs to have its likelihood of occurrence determined, and the likely severity.

Then, the likelihood multiplied by the severity gives you your risk score.

Risk: Pro Tip!

Risk is all about business impact. Once you know your risks, you know what to do to get rid of them... and how to deal with a crisis.

Risk Thinking

Risk Likelihood

The likelihood scores are dependent on your publishing frequency. If you publish once per month or less, then your risk rating needs to be different from a firm that publishes twice every week.

5 = Almost certain

4 = Likely, has occurred before

3 = Possible (1 occurrence in 10 years)

2 = Unlikely (1 occurrence in 3 years)

1 = Rare (has never occurred, can't see when it might)

Risk Severity

The severity scores are dependent on how you foresee business impact. If you are working in a high risk area anyway, such as one in which breaching compliance requirements has very significant impacts, then your severity ratings will be less forgiving.

1 = Minor business impact (<$5k), minor compliance issues

2 = Minimal business impact ($5k to $10k), compliance breach

3 = Substantial business impact ($10k to $100k), regulation breach

4 = Significant business impact, major breach, facing litigation

5 = Major business impact, facing prosecution, facing customer litigation action

Create a risk register

A risk register is the only way you can effectively manage your risk. You will find a template for your risk register on the following pages. You may choose to use an expanded version, which gives you more visibility - such as on a spreadsheet.

Excellent risk registers include:

- the last review date
- how the risk is being controlled or minimised
- an assessment of that control's effectiveness
- whether or not the risk is acceptable ...
- and so on.

Then what should I do?

Once you've discovered and rated all of your risks, work out the best way to remove, control, or mitigate them. Some of those may require establishment of rules or guidelines.

Knowing the actions that must be taken to remove or mitigate risks gives you the basis on which to form a strong internal system for checks and balances. Paired with your WRACI Matrix, the risk register gives you the capacity to assign responsibility and accountabilities, and then to measure the effectiveness of your risk management.

Once you have done this monumental amount of work, you can really start moving forwards.

Risk Thinking

Risk Likelihood

Score	Likelihood	Your definition
1	Rare	
2	Unlikely	
3	Possible	
4	Likely	
5	Almost Certain	

Risk Severity

Score	Severity	Your definition
1	Low	
2	Minor	
3	Medium	
4	High	
5	Very High	

TOTAL RISK SCORE = Likelihood x Severity

Risk Thinking

Publishing Risk Register

Date of last review: _____

Reviewed by: _____

Risk	Likelihood	Severity	SCORE	How we control it

Risk Ratings

LOW	1 - 4	Take immediate action to remove or
MEDIUM	5 - 8	control all very high and high risks.
HIGH	9 - 19	Act on remaining risks in descending
VERY HIGH	20+	order of severity.

Plan to make it happen

No publishing ever happened without a plan. Or rather, it did. But it stopped. It happened when people were inspired and excited, and it stopped when nothing went to plan.

☺☺☺☺☺☺☺☺☺☺
🕐 2 mins   📋 15 mins   ✏ 60 mins

If you are hoping your blog will be successful, you need to be aware that hope is not a plan. A plan is a plan. Establish an editorial calendar before you write a word. Then, put the dates and timeframes in everyone's diaries, and your life will be much easier because the up-front thinking is already done.

How to create a fantastic editorial calendar

You have two options. You could:

- Start from scratch using the guideline below
- Use the free template at http://bit.ly/FreeCalendarTemplate.

Minimum requirements for your editorial calendar

Proposed title

Description

Length

Draft date

Subject-matter expert approval date

Editorial review date

Publishing date.

Schedule everything

Once your editorial calendar is complete and signed-off, schedule everything. Right now, this kind of scheduling feels unnecessary. But it's like leaving washed dishes in the drying rack: The dishes are done, but the job isn't finished.

Scheduling time to write, time to approve, time to publish - or whatever your responsibility is - will make sure that it happens.

If you don't have the right security level to add dates or events to other people's calendars, hold a meeting for the purpose of booking everything in.

Planning: Pro Tip!

Complete your editorial calendar for an entire year. You already have your topics defined: You know who is going to write them. Completing your editorial calendar will be easy. Make sure it covers a full year!

Writing for a web-based audience

Writing for a public, web-based audience means using a specific structure, and being aware of how people read (or, rather, scan) online.

🕐 **3 mins** 📋 **0 mins** ✏️ **5 mins**

Deep reading doesn't happen online.

According to studies of high-literacy users, readers of web pages read, on average, 20% of a page.[1] It is likely to be lower for those who aren't university educated.

Reference:
[1] https://www.nngroup.com/articles/how-little-do-users-read/

The structure is different

What this means for you is that your articles and pages must be short, clear and succinct. The flow needs to be clear. Headings and navigational 'pointers' must also be clear.

It also means that you need to have a summary at the top of every page.

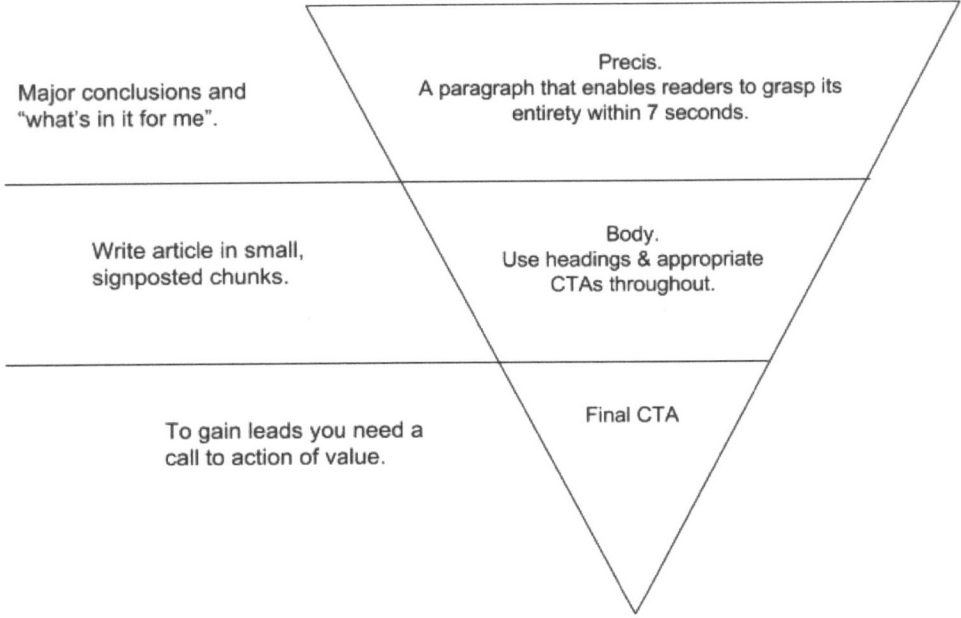

Major conclusions and "what's in it for me".

Precis.
A paragraph that enables readers to grasp its entirety within 7 seconds.

Write article in small, signposted chunks.

Body.
Use headings & appropriate CTAs throughout.

To gain leads you need a call to action of value.

Final CTA

Writing for a web-based audience

Signpost your article with headings

In print, you can run-on text without headings to point out every major argument or change. It's not the same online. For a scanning reader, you want to make grasping the whole as simple as possible. That means lots of headings

Great headings aren't just markers. They support your precis, and help a scanning reader to see that what you promise to deliver you actually deliver.

Many readers "bounce' out of articles because what they see isn't what was promised on the tin, so to speak.

Make it easy to read

Complexity is the greatest stumbling block in the legal profession's ability to relate to its publics. Lawyers write and speak very differently from everyone else. They use the complicated versions of words, in structures unfamiliar to everyone else.

Language that is consistently simple and user-oriented presents fewer barriers for your clients and not-yet-clients. It is also an element that can be quantitatively measured.

Always assess the simplicity of your work

This check needs to be part of your editorial review, for every single article.

- Copy the text of your blog or other article
- Check its readability by going to Hemingway App, which you can find at http://hemingwayapp.com
- Repeat for every other article.
- Your ideal score should be at about Grade 8 or 9 for every single item.

Suggested Readability Score Tolerances

Corporate Law = Up to Grade 10

Family Law = Maximum Grade 8

Criminal Law = Maximum Grade 8

Constitutional Law = Up to Grade 14

Environmental Law = Up to Grade 9

Establish your own readability score tolerances, with the reasons included.

This gives your team non-arbitrary, testable measures.

MYTH: Complexity = Wisdom or Learning

It is widely believed that complexity is an indication of wisdom or learning. In fact, the opposite is true. Needless complexity (meaning, you haven't attempted to simplify it for a non-expert audience) is an indication that you don't understand your topic well enough to write it for them.

FREE Simplicity Model: http://bit.ly/SimplicityModel

Use meaningful images

Any images, figures, or charts that you add to your blogs need to add meaning to the article, or support its argument in some way.

☺ ☺ ☺ ☺ ☺ ☺ ☺ ☺ ☺ ☺

🕐 **1 mins**　📋 **0 mins**　✎ **Depends on requirements**

The difficulty that you face is trying to include up to three images for every article depending on its length.

That seems like a lot of images only if you assume you can't re-use them. You can! In fact, it's necessary to have the freedom to re-use media assets if you are going to have a lean, fast-moving publishing structure.

Build an image library that supports your strategic direction

Like written content, image, film, and audio content needs to support your strategic direction. If it does, then you will be able to use it and re-use it.

Wherever possible, have photographers take the photographs for you, or commission the artwork. You can use stock images, but they look cheap and tend to be less meaningful.

Make sure that all charts and figures are legible, and avoid colour combinations that make life difficult for colour-blind readers.

All images must have alt text

Not everyone will see the images that you add. Anyone using a screen reader, anyone in an area with slow internet, or anyone with image blockers turned on will see your alternative text instead.

Alternative text should, like the image, add meaning.

If the image is a chart or a figure, any text (or ultimate conclusion) needs to be in the alternative text too.

Help readers of all abilities, and with all types of technology, to get the maximum benefit of reading your work.

> ### Images: Pro Tip!
>
> If you don't have a photographer (or budget), use only Creative Commons licensed images. Great resources are:
>
> Pexels: http://pexels.com
> Unsplash: http://unsplash.com

You can now get started!

Congratulations, you've reached the point where you can get started. If you have completed every activity in this playbook before you got here, then you now have a fully functioning, high performance publishing system.

It's up to you to keep it going.

☺ ☺ ☺ ☺ ☺ ☺ ☺ ☺ ☺ ☺

🕐 0 mins   📋 0 mins   ✏️ 0 mins

Stay in front

Following the principles in this playbook, take the time to review your system's performance.

This means:

- Schedule time to review your metrics.
- If something needs adjusting, adjust it immediately.
- Schedule time to measure how well your system is performing to keep your competitive position unique, which means running a minor competitive analysis at least annually
- Schedule time to establish your next year's publishing, adjusted to account for any changes you've identified in topics, readerships, or offers.

Want help or advice? Free support

At Brutal Pixie, our intention is to make communication human, with empathy, support, and encouragement. This is why we provide free support to all firms who purchase this playbook.

How to access your free support

Call +61 8 8121 4134 or email hello@brutalpixie.com with the subject: Playbook Support.

In your email, tell us your name, the firm you work for, and the issue you need help with.

We'll get back to you within 48 hours.
For free.

Brutal Pixie provides a range of services to the legal profession, including content strategy, risk management, training, content creation, and much more.

Learn more about us at http://brutalpixie.com